THE SECRET OF
BROTHERLY LOVE

THE SECRET OF
BROTHERLY LOVE

Andrew Murray

PUBLICATIONS

Fort Washington, PA 19034

The Secret of Brotherly Love
Published by CLC Publications

U.S.A.
P.O. Box 1449, Fort Washington, PA 19034

UNITED KINGDOM
CLC International (UK)
Unit 5, Glendale Avenue, Sandycroft, Flintshire, CH5 2QP

ISBN (paperback): 978-1-61958-278-1
ISBN (e-book): 978-1-61958-279-8

Unless otherwise noted, all Scripture quotations are from the Holy Bible, New King James Version, copyright © 1979, 1980, 1982 by Thomas Nelson, Inc. Used by permission. All rights reserved.

Italics in Scripture quotations are the emphasis of the author.

Cover design by Mitch Bolton.

INTRODUCTION

The subject of Love, with which this little book deals, is one of the most difficult and profound of themes. It is no easy task to ascend to heaven and there behold the heavenly glory as an ocean of holy, all-embracing love! . . . and then to return to earth and here see how, among men, instead of brotherliness, hatred, with all its sad results, has characterized the history of mankind. Yes, and it reached its climax in the rejection and crucifixion of the eternal love embodied in the person of the Lord Jesus Christ.

Think of the state of the world at present, and then consider the power that the Evil One has to divide even God's children from each other in sometimes bitter enmity. What a task it is to reconcile God's everlasting Father-love and the sad strife seen among brethren. How difficult it becomes to recommend this love so as to find for it an entrance into men's hearts! How shall we, above all, persuade God's children that living in the love of God and in love to the brethren is not only *possible* but a plain *duty*, and worth the sacrifice of all to possess and to proclaim it?

At times I have felt as though I must give up writing this little book. People will not believe that it is possible, through God's Holy Spirit, to be so filled with the love of God and of the Lord Christ that love as streams of living water shall flow forth from them. They will not believe that God's Word speaks the absolute truth when it says: "In all these things we are more than conquerors through Him who loved us" (Rom. 8:37); "[Nothing] shall be able to separate us from the love of God which is in Christ Jesus our Lord" (8:39).

And yet I felt compelled to write, for the Word of God is living and powerful and abides forever. I came to see, as never before, how inseparably faith in Christ and love to the brethren are bound together. New light was shed on the text: "This is His commandment: that we should believe on the name of His Son Jesus Christ and love one another, as He gave us commandment" (1 John 3:23).

But chiefly I have gained fresh insight into the reason for such a lack of love to God, and of love to the brethren and all mankind. Many a Christian wearies himself in the attempt to love always, for so often he fails. And the reason for this failure is simply that we have no power in ourselves to love even *God* (much less our brethren or our enemies) "because the carnal mind is enmity against God; for it is not subject to the law of God, nor indeed can be" (Rom. 8:7). Our old nature—the old Man—loves to do its *own* will and to gratify its sinful desires. To love the great and holy God; to love Christ, who first loved us; to love our brethren and our enemies, is impossible to the carnal mind. Such love is not in ourselves! We can only receive it from above—when we cast ourselves down before God with a sense of our own helplessness and unworthiness, that He may fill us.

When a Christian comes to understand that the love wherewith God and Christ love him should be in him too—and not merely as a pleasant experience but as a divine life-power, *abiding* in him—he can have assurance that the Spirit of God longs to effect this love in him. And as he believes this, and surrenders himself fully to the Holy Spirit, he will find that he *can* and *will* love all men.

This truth having taken possession of me anew, I feel that I must pass it on to others. "The love of God," with which we may love Him and our fellow men, "has been poured out in our hearts by the Holy Spirit" (Rom 5:5). Yes, the fruit of the Spirit is love—which includes all the long-suffering and kindness and goodness and patience needed in our association with our fellow men (see Gal. 5:22–23).

Because I fully believe this, I invite my readers to adore the love of God with me, and the miracles of grace it can work in human hearts—filling them with divine love.

Let us worship God and wait upon Him to pour out this love in our hearts so that streams of blessing may flow from us to a needy world.

Your servant in the Lord,
ANDREW MURRAY

Love and Faith

This is His commandment: that we should believe on the name of His Son Jesus Christ and love one another, as He gave us commandment.

First John 3:23

AT a conference at Graaff-Reinet, the closing service was held on Sunday night. At the afternoon meeting we speakers decided to take as our subject the five great lessons to be learned from the parable of the Vine and Branches in John 15. The subject of brotherly love fell to the lot of a certain minister. But he demurred, saying: "I cannot speak on that subject for I have never yet preached on it." In explanation, he said: "You know that I studied in Holland, and when there the subject of love was left to the liberal section. They did not believe in God's stern justice, nor in redemption through Christ. God was *love*; that was enough! The orthodox party were not allowed to suggest that their opponents should be put out of the church. No, all should be borne in love! And so it came to pass that the orthodox party were strong in preaching faith but left the preaching of love to the liberal section."

The church must learn not only to preach the love of God in redemption, it must go further and teach Christians to show that the love of Christ is in their hearts. How? By love shown to the brethren. Our Lord called this a new commandment: a badge by which the world would recognize His disciples!

There is a great need for this preaching of love. God sometimes allows bitterness to arise between Christians in order that they may view the terrible power of sin in their hearts and shrink back at the sight. How greatly a minister and his people should feel the importance of Christ's command: "Love one another." A life of great holiness will result if we really love each other as Christ loves us.

May the reading of this booklet help us to understand the two manifestations of love: the wonderful love of God in Christ to us, and the wonderful reciprocal love in us, through the Holy Spirit, to Him and to our brethren.

Faith and Love

And the grace of our Lord was exceedingly abundant, with faith and love.

First Timothy 1:14

Your work of faith [and] labor of love.

First Thessalonians 1:3

The breastplate of faith and love.

First Thessalonians 5:8

Your faith grows exceedingly, and the love of every one of you all abounds toward each other.

Second Thessalonians 1:3

THESE expressions by the apostle Paul show us the true connection between faith and love in the life of a Christian. Faith always comes first; it roots itself deeply in the love of God, and bears fruit in love to the brethren. As in nature the root and the fruit are inseparable, so is it with faith and love in the realm of grace.

Too often the two are separated. On the day of Pentecost they were one: there was a powerful faith towards the Lord Jesus joined with a fervent love to the brethren. The sum of the preaching on that day was: "Repent and believe in the name of Jesus Christ, and you will receive the gift of the Holy Spirit." And the natural result followed: "Now all who believed were together, and had all things in common" (Acts 2:44); "Now the multitude of those who believed were of one heart and one soul" (4:32).

Alas, that this should not have been wholly the case at the Reformation. A powerful reawakening took place in regard to the doctrine of faith, but at the same time what a lack of love there was between many of the preachers and leaders in that faith! So the world was not taught the lesson that God's love was all-powerful and able to sanctify the whole life of man.

Let this thought sink deep into our hearts: "The grace of our Lord was exceedingly abundant, with faith and love" (1 Tim 1:14). As we cultivate *faith in God's love*, our hearts will be *filled with love to the brethren*. The genuineness of our faith regarding the love of God toward us must be shown by love in our daily lives at home.

May God help us from day to day by faith to be *rooted* in this love, that we may at all times be living examples of its truth and power and so become a blessing to others.

The Love of God

*God is love, and he who abides in love abides in God, and
God in him.*

First John 4:16

MAY God through His Holy Spirit grant us grace
rightly to adore this unfathomable mystery.

Jesus said: "No one is good but One, that is, God"
(Luke 18:19). The glory of God in heaven is that He has
a will to be and do all that is good. That includes the two
meanings of the word: *good*, all that is right and perfect;
good, all that makes happy.

The God who wills nothing but good is a God of
love. He does not seek His own: He does not live for
Himself, but pours out His love on all living creatures.
All created things share in this love, to the end that they
may be satisfied with that which is good.

The characteristic of love is that it "does not seek its
own" (1 Cor. 13:5). It finds its happiness in giving to
others; it sacrifices itself wholly for others. Even so God
offered *Himself* to mankind in the person of His Son,
and the Son offered Himself upon the cross to bring
that love to men and to win their hearts. The everlasting
love with which the Father loved the Son is the same
love with which the Son has loved us. This self-same
love of God, Christ has poured into our hearts through
the Holy Spirit so that our whole life may be permeated
with its vital power.

The love of God to His Son, the love of the Son to us, the love with which we love the Son, the love with which we, in obedience to His command, love the brethren, and try to love all men and win them for Christ—all is the same eternal, incomprehensible, almighty love of God! Love is the power of the Godhead, in the Father, Son, and Holy Spirit. This love is the possession of all who are members of the body of Christ and streams forth from them to take the whole world into its compass.

Unsearchable, adorable wonder of love! "He who abides in love abides in God, and God in him." Oh my soul, meditate on this wondrous love and adore the great God of Love!

The Love of Christ

For the love of Christ compels us.

Second Corinthians 5:14

GOD sent His Son into the world to make known His everlasting love, even as it was known in heaven. God's existence there is enveloped in the glory of that love: all His angels are as tongues of fire overflowing with praise and worship through the power of the love that fills them. God's desire is that on this sinful earth, likewise, His love should take possession of the hearts of men.

And how was this to be accomplished? By sending Christ, the Son of His love, to earth to reveal as Man the love of the Father and win our hearts to Himself. The Lord Jesus became man and made Himself of no reputation. In His dealings with the poor and needy, and those who were unbelieving and rebellious, and through His gracious miracles, He poured out His love into the hearts of sinful men.

With the same purpose our Lord chose the disciples to be always with Him and to be filled with His love. With this purpose He then gave, on the cross, the greatest proof of love that the world has ever seen. He took our sins upon Himself. He suffered and bore the scorn of His enemies that friend and foe alike might know God's eternal love.

And then, after He had ascended to heaven, He gave the Holy Spirit to pour out this love in our hearts. The disciples, impelled by the love of Christ, in turn offered their lives to make it known to others.

Oh Christians, think this over: God longs to have our hearts wholly filled with His love. Then He will be able to use us as channels for this love to flow out to our fellow men. Let us say with the apostle Paul: "The love of Christ compels me (Dutch Version—"urges"). I can be satisfied with nothing less. I will sacrifice everything to secure a place for this great love in the hearts of the children of men."

The Love of the Spirit

*The love of God has been poured out in our hearts by the
Holy Spirit who was given to us.*

Romans 5:5

HOW many a Christian must confess that he knows very little of an open-hearted, fervent, childlike love to his heavenly Father! He realizes, too, that he cannot keep Christ's second great commandment, to love his neighbor as himself. The thought of this lack of a joyful love to the Lord Jesus, or of a continual love to the brethren, is a great source of shame and sorrow.

What is the cause of this failure? Has the heavenly Father made no provision for His children on earth, enabling them to prove their love to Him and to each other? Certainly He has. But God's children have not learned the lesson that there must be a constant renewal of faith in what God is able to do. One tries to stir up love towards God in one's heart, yet is conscious all the time that in one's own strength a person cannot awaken the slightest love to God. Oh Christian, believe that the love of God will work in your heart as a vital power to enable you to love God and to love the brethren. Cease to expect the least love in yourself. Believe in the power of God's love, resting on you and abiding in you; teaching you to love God, and the brethren, with His own love.

Learn the lesson of our text: "The love of God has been poured out in our hearts by the Holy Spirit."

The Spirit will enable us to love God and our brethren, and even our enemies. Be assured of two things. First, that in your own strength you cannot love God or the brethren. And, second, that the Holy Spirit is within you every day and every hour, seeking to fill you with the spirit of love. Each morning, as you commit yourself into the keeping of the Holy Spirit for the day, let this prayer arise: Grant me the assurance that You will pour forth the love of Christ into my own heart, and then let it stream forth to all around me!

The Power of Love

We are more than conquerors through Him who loved us.
Romans 8:37

IN days of unrest and strong racial feeling, we need above all a new discovery and living experience of the love of God. Let us anchor our hope in the thought that "God is love" (1 John 4:16). God's power, by which He rules and guides the world, is the power of an undying, persistent love. He works through the hearts and spirits and wills of men and women wholly yielded to Him and His service; and He waits for them to open their hearts to Him in love and then, full of courage, to become witnesses for Him.

When this has been achieved, Christ's kingdom is manifested and His reign of love on earth begun. Christ died in order to establish this kingdom. The only means He used to gain influence was through the manifestation of a great serving, suffering love. He saw the possibility of redemption in the hearts of even the worst of men. He knew that men's hearts could never resist the steady, continuous influence of love; and that unbounded faith in God's love would be our strength and stay. It was in the fire and the fervor of that love that the disciples were able to expect, and to do, the impossible.

The spirit of hatred and bitterness can never be overcome by argument or by reproaches. Some think things can never be different, but if we really believe in the omnipotence of God's love we may not distrust His power. God's children must learn to accept His love, not only for themselves individually but for the life of others. Gradually better feelings will prevail if believers will yield themselves unreservedly for God to work through them. Our faith in love as the greatest power in the world should prepare us for a life in communion with God in prayer and for a life of unselfish service among our fellow men. Let each Christian examine his life and pray for grace, as a servant of that all-powerful love, to live for those around him.

The Sign of a True Church

*By this all will know that you are My disciples, if you have
love for one another.*

John 13:35

WE are taught in most of our creeds that the true
church is to be found where God's Word is rightly
preached and the holy sacraments dispensed, as instituted
by Christ. Christ Himself took a much broader view. Not
merely what the church teaches through her ministers
was, to Him, the distinguishing mark of His followers,
but a life lived in love to the brethren.

It is most important that we should understand
this. In God, love reaches its highest point and is the
culmination of His glory. In the man Christ Jesus on
the cross, love is at its highest. We owe everything to
this love. Love is the power that moved Jesus to die for
us. In love, God highly exalted Him as Lord and Christ.
Love is the power that broke our hearts, and love is the
power that heals them. Love is the power through which
Christ dwells in us and works in us. Love can change my
whole nature and enable me to surrender all to God. It
gives me strength to live a holy, joyous life, full of blessing to others. Every Christian should show forth, as in
a mirror, the love of God.

Alas, how seldom do Christians realize this! They
seek, in the power of human love, to love Christ and the
brethren. And then they fail. They are sure it is impossible

to lead such a life, and they do not even greatly desire it or pray for it. They do not understand that we may and can love with God's own love, which is poured forth unto our hearts by the Holy Spirit.

Oh, that this great truth might possess us: the love of God is poured out in our hearts *by the Holy Spirit*. If we fully believe that the Holy Spirit, dwelling within us, will maintain this heavenly love from hour to hour, we shall be able to understand the word of Christ: "All things are possible to him who believes" (Mark 9:23), and to love God and Christ with all our hearts; and, what is even harder, to love our brethren, and even our enemies, while love flows from us as a stream of living water "through the Holy Spirit."

Race-Hatred

*For we ourselves were also once foolish . . . living in malice
and envy, hateful and hating one another.*

Titus 3:3

WHAT a dark picture of the state of human nature and of human society! Whence comes such a sad condition of things, worse even than we see among animals? The answer is: "From Adam's fall." Just think how Cain, the first child born on earth, born of man whom God had created, shed the blood of his brother Abel. Yes, the first child born on earth was the murderer of his own brother, and came under the power of the devil who "was a murderer from the beginning" (John 8:44); "Then the LORD saw that the wickedness of man was great in the earth, and that every intent of the thoughts of his heart was only evil continually" (Gen. 6:5). No wonder that He destroyed mankind by a flood. Yet soon after the flood there were signs that man was still under the power of sin.

Prayer is like fire. The fire can only burn brightly if it is supplied with good fuel. That fuel is God's Word, which must not only be studied carefully and prayerfully but must be taken into the heart and lived out in the life. The inspiration and powerful working of the Holy Spirit alone can do this.

No wonder that man's love of his own people, implanted in his heart by nature, soon changed to hatred of other peoples. Love of country became the fruitful source of race-hatred, war, and bloodshed. Note how, here in South Africa, God has placed the two races side by side, as in a school, to see if our Christianity will enable us to overcome race-hatred and, in the power of Christ's love, prove that in the new creature "there is neither Greek nor Jew, circumcised nor uncircumcised, barbarian, Scythian, slave nor free, but Christ is all and in all" (Col. 3:11).

What an opening there is for the church of Christ and her ministers to preach and proclaim the love of God, and to prove its might to change race-hatred into brotherly love! God has abundant power to bring this to pass.

What a call to every Christian to pray for himself and his brethren, that we may not make the Word of God ineffectual by our unbelief!

Oh God, make known to us Your love in heavenly power, and let it take full possession of our lives!

Love Your Enemies
Me No' Love Fingo!

*You have heard that it was said, "You shall love your neighbor
and hate your enemy."*

Matthew 5:43

IT was the Jewish rabbis in Christ's earthly day who said
this. They deemed they had a right to say it because of
what was written in Leviticus 19:17–18: "You shall not
hate your brother in your heart. You shall surely rebuke
your neighbor, and not bear sin because of him. You
shall not take vengeance, nor bear any grudge against
the children of your people, but you shall love your
neighbor as yourself." From this they argued that it was
only the children of their own people whom they might
not hate; it was all right to hate their enemies. But our
Lord said: "Love your enemies, bless those who curse
you" (Matt. 5:44)

How often the Christian follows the example of
the Jewish teachers! The command of our Lord is too
strict and narrow for him; he has not yielded himself to
God in obedience to the new commandment to love his
brethren with Christ's love, believing that this love will
flow out to all around, even to those who hate us. This
will require much grace, and will cost time and trouble
and much earnest prayer.

When I was a minister in Cape Town, I met a Ger-
man deaconess who was working in connection with

the English church at Woodstock. She had a class every evening for ten or twelve Kaffirs who were preparing for admission to the church. One evening she spoke about loving our enemies. She asked one man if his people had enemies. "Oh yes!" "Who are they?" "The Fingoes." (The Kaffirs count the Fingoes as dogs.) She asked the man if he could love a Fingo. His answer was quite decided: "Me no' love Fingo! Me no' love Fingo!" It was an indisputable fact; there could be no question about it. He could not love a Fingo. She told him that in that case he could not go to the Communion. He went home very thoughtful, and the next evening at class seemed very downcast. But he still had only one answer: "Me no' love Fingo!" He was not received into the church with the others, but continued to attend the class. He was always in earnest, and there was evidently a struggle going on; until one evening he appeared with a bright face and said: "Me *now* love Fingo!" He had prayed about it, and God had heard his prayer.

There is only one way to love our enemies; by the love of Christ, sought and found in prayer.

Forgive, but Not Forget

I will forgive their iniquity, and their sin I will remember no more.

Jeremiah 31:34

AT the unveiling of the Women's Monument at Bloemfontein in 1913, I happened to be sitting in the front row on the platform at the foot of the monument. After a while the sun became very hot. Suddenly I noticed that someone behind me was holding an umbrella over my head. When the speaker had finished, I asked my nephew beside me: "Who is so friendly as to hold an umbrella over my head?" His answer was: "General de Wet." I was surprised, and turning around, thanked him heartily. My nephew told me afterwards that he had said: "But I would gladly have paid for the privilege of doing it." I thought, what a generous nature to speak in that way. Presently the General's turn came to give an address. I could agree with all he said except his last words, which were: "Forgive—yes; but forget—never." When the ceremony was over and I shook hands with him again, it was in my heart to say to him: "You say, 'I can never forget.' Be careful to what that may lead."

Many a one has allowed himself to be deceived by these words. On the farms, I have often seen a dog come in at the front door to seek coolness and shade. He would be driven out and the door closed. Then he would go through the back door, and would soon be inside the house again. The front door represents: "I will forgive." One wishes to put away all thought of hatred or ill-feeling. But see how quickly and quietly these evil thoughts come back through the back door of "I will never forget." Many a one trusts in God's forgiving love, but does not remember that when God forgives, He forgets. "I will forgive their iniquity, and their sin I will remember no more." And St. Paul gives us the advice in Colossians 3:13: "Forgiving one another . . . even as Christ forgave you, so you also must do."

As God Forgives

And forgive us our sins, for we also forgive everyone who is indebted to us.

Luke 11:4

THE forgiveness of sins is the great all-embracing gift by which, in His mercy, God sets the sinner free and receives him back into His love and favor. The forgiveness of sins is the fount of our salvation and gives us boldness towards God. The forgiveness of sins gives us cause for thankfulness every day of our lives. It is God's will—and our souls feel the need of it—that we should each day walk with Him as those whose sins are forgiven and who are living in the light of His countenance.

As we walk with God in the full assurance of sins forgiven, He desires that in our contacts with our fellow men, too, we should live as those who have been freely forgiven. And we can prove our sincerity only by forgiving those who have offended us as freely and as willingly as God has forgiven us.

How clearly and urgently our Lord speaks upon this! In the Lord's Prayer we are taught to pray each day: "Forgive us our debts, as we forgive our debtors" (Matt. 6:12), and then at the end: "If you do not forgive men their trespasses, neither will your Father forgive your trespasses" (6:15). After the great promise of Mark 11:24 come the words: "And whenever you stand praying, if you have anything against anyone, forgive him."

In Matthew 18:21 we have the question of Peter: "Lord, how often shall my brother sin against me, and I forgive him?" and our Lord's answer: "Up to seventy times seven." Then follows the parable of the servant whose lord forgave him his debt, but who would not show compassion on his fellow servant. His lord's question to him was: "Should you not also have had compassion on your fellow servant, just as I had pity on you?" (18:33). So he was delivered to the jailer. And our Lord gives the warning: "So My heavenly Father also will do to you if each of you, from his heart, does not forgive his brother" (18:35).

Let us remember to realize daily: As I need God's forgiveness each day, so let me be ready each day to forgive my brother. God grant us grace to do it!

The Preaching of Love

The greatest of these is love.

First Corinthians 13:13

DURING the Boer War, when there was much unrest in the country, a certain minister asked his brother-minister, who was a leader in the church, to do his best to calm the minds of those around him. His answer was: "I have enough trouble with myself. My own mind is unsettled; how can I quiet others?" If there were a revival of the preaching of love, more than one of our ministers would have to say: "There is such a lack of love in my own heart; how can I teach others?"

Yet there is a remedy. Let me tell you what I have learned from John Wesley. During the first fourteen years of his ministry he had no insight into what a free and full salvation by faith meant. After he had been convicted of the sin of unbelief, by means of a conversation with one of the Moravian Brethren, he began to preach with such power that many were converted. But he felt that it was too much a matter of the intellect; he had not yet experienced the full joy and love which the Moravian possessed. He asked the brother what he should do. The answer was: "Preach it because you believe that it is what God's Word teaches. You will soon find what you are seeking, and will then preach it because you possess it."

This has been my own experience. Often in preaching, or in writing, I have asked myself: But do you possess what you preach to others? And I have followed the advice: Preach it because you believe it to be the teaching of God's Word and heartily desire it. Preach the truth by faith, and the experience will follow.

Let the minister who feels impelled to preach about love not hesitate to do so, and he will soon be able to preach it because he has himself received that which he commends.

The Two Leaders

Therefore I exhort first of all that supplications, prayers, intercessions, and giving of thanks be made for all men, for kings and all who are in authority, that we may lead a quiet and peaceable life in all godliness and reverence.

First Timothy 2:1–2

AT the time of the unveiling of the Women's Monument at Bloemfontein, before the procession took place, I spoke a few words in the Dutch church about the suffering, praying, all-conquering love of these women who, they say, prayed earnestly that God would keep them from hatred or want of love towards their enemies. I expressed the hope that this prayerful love might be ours, and that nothing might be done to disturb the feeling of peace and unity. I said that there were some who feared disunion not only between the two races in the country but between those who were fellow countrymen. Not long after, we heard that there had been a breach between the leaders of the two parties.

I felt impelled to write an article on the question: "For whom do you pray?" Someone answers: "I pray for the man at the head of the government, and who, under God's guidance, as general of the burghers in the war, has now become the leader of all South Africa. I pray for him." And another: "I pray especially for the man who has been serviceable in bringing the interests of his people into the foreground." But would it not be sad if we came into God's presence divided into two camps, praying one against the other? No, we must pray for *both* our leaders, and for *all* who are in authority. As leaders of the people, their influence for good or evil is inexpressible. Their hearts are in God's hands, and He can turn them wherever He wills. Let our prayers ascend to God in all sincerity, and He will hear and grant that which is good for the whole land. Let us pray: "Lord, the hearts of rulers are in Your hands; teach them to do Your will."

Unfeigned Love of the Brethren

Since you have purified your souls in obeying the truth through the Spirit in sincere love of the brethren, love one another fervently with a pure heart.

First Peter 1:22

IN the beginning of this chapter, Peter had expressed a wonderful truth about our love to Christ: "Whom having not seen you love. Though now you do not see Him, yet believing, you rejoice with joy inexpressible and full of glory" (1 Pet. 1:8). This was the fruit of the Spirit.

In our text he speaks of "the love of the brethren." "You have purified your souls in obeying the truth through the Spirit in sincere love of the brethren." In the days of the early church it was clearly understood at conversion that, in confessing Christ, the new convert also promised sincere love to the brethren. So Peter continues: "Love one another fervently with a pure heart" (1:22). Unfeigned, fervent love through the Spirit should be the chief token of a true conversion.

We see how much stress Peter lays on this point in the next three chapters, as he returns to the subject each time. In 2:17—"Love the brotherhood. Fear God. Honor the king." At 3:8—"Finally, all of you be of one mind, having compassion for one another; love as brothers, be tenderhearted, be courteous." These are all signs of the life of God in the soul. And then (4:7–8), "Be serious and watchful in your prayers. And above all things have fervent love for one another, for 'love will cover a multitude of sins.'" Unfeigned, fervent love of the brethren was the indispensable sign of true godliness.

God's Word is a mirror into which the church and each individual member must look to see that we are truly Christian, showing by our conduct that we take God's Word as our rule of life. If our hearts condemn us, we must turn at once to God, confessing our sin. Let us believe that the Spirit of love does indeed dwell in us, and will pour out God's love in our hearts and purify us from all hatred and selfishness and restore the image of Christ within us. Let us not rest content until we have surrendered ourselves wholly to God, that His Spirit of love may reign and rule within us.

Day 15

The Spirit of Love

The fruit of the Spirit is love.

Galatians 5:22

God has . . . given us a spirit . . . of love.

Second Timothy 1:7

OUR love, which is the fruit of the Spirit, does not consist merely in the knowledge of, and faith in, God's love as revealed in our redemption. No, the matter goes far deeper. Our love has its origin in the fact that the love of God has been poured out in our hearts by the Holy Spirit—not only as an experience or feeling, but the spirit of love takes possession of us and directs and controls and inspires. This love becomes a heavenly life-power, a disposition of the soul whereby man tastes and knows that God is good. The Spirit gives to love such a form that it contains the commands of the divine love within itself, and thus can keep the commandments without difficulty. "For this is the love of God, that we keep His commandments. And His commandments are not burdensome" (1 John 5:3). When God, according to promise, writes His law in our hearts, the summing up of that law is love. It governs the life of the man wholly devoted to God and controls his thoughts and actions.

This divine love in the heart of man is as a little sanctuary from which the child of God receives power, in obedience to the inner law of love, to live always in the love of God. This holy love includes fellowship with God, union with Christ, and love to the brethren.

How can we attain to this experience? Through faith alone. The chief sign of faith in the blind and the lepers who came to Christ to be healed was the knowledge of their own impotence and inability to help themselves. When our eyes have been opened and we realize that the love of God has already been poured out in our hearts by His Spirit, enabling us to keep His commandments and to love the brethren—then let us bow in stillness of soul before God and adore the love which has taken possession of our hearts, until our faith can firmly say: God has indeed given me the spirit of love in my heart. In the power of the Spirit I can and will love God and my fellow men.

A Song of Love

And now abide faith, hope, love, these three; but the greatest of these is love.

First Corinthians 13:13

THIS chapter is wholly devoted to the praise of love. The first three verses speak of the absolute necessity of love as the chief thing in our religion. "Though I speak with the tongues of men and of angels," "And though I have the gift of prophecy, and understand all mysteries and all knowledge," "And though I have all faith, so that I could remove mountains," "And though I bestow all my goods to feed the poor, and though I give my body to be burned, but have not love"—then, three times repeated, "I have become sounding brass or a clanging cymbal," "I am nothing," "It profits me nothing" (1 Cor. 13:1–3).

If I have not love, it all profits me nothing.

Then follows the Song of Love (13:4–8). There are fifteen things said about love—what it is and what it is not. In this description one sentence sums up the whole nature of love: Love "does not seek its own." And again: "Love never fails." Prophecies, tongues, and knowledge shall vanish away. Even faith and hope shall be changed into sight. But love abides to all eternity, as long as God endures. Love is the greatest thing in the world.

We should read this chapter oftener than we do, and commit the Song to memory, so that the great words are imprinted on our hearts: Love "does not seek its own."

Think over it and pray over it. "Love never fails." Consider all that means. "The greatest of these is love." Let this love rule in your life.

God is love. "He who abides in love abides in God, and God in him" (1 John 4:16). Oh Christian, are you living in a world that is uncharitable and selfish, full of bitterness and hatred? Take refuge under the wings of this everlasting love. Let your heart be filled with it, so that by God's almighty power you may be a witness to the transforming power of love. Thus you will be a fountain of blessing to all around you.

Live each day in fellowship with the triune love of Father, Son, and Holy Spirit, and you will learn the secret of how to love.

The Obedience of Love

If you love Me, keep My commandments.

John 14:15

THE love wherewith the Father loved the Son was a wonderful, never-ending love. All that the Father was and had, He gave to the Son. The Son responded to this love by giving the Father all. Cost what it might, He kept the Father's commandments and abode in His love.

Christ, in His great love to us, sacrificed all; His life and death were wholly at our service. And He asks of us only that which is reasonable: that we, out of love, should keep His commandments. Read verses 15, 21, 23, and see how the words are repeated three times, together with the great promise that follows. And chapter 15 verses 7, 10, 14 speak three times of the rich blessing connected with the keeping of the commandments.

"If you love Me, keep My commandments." This precept loses its power because Christians say: "It is quite impossible: I cannot always keep His commandments." And so conscience is quieted and the commands are not kept. Yet our Lord really meant it, for in the last night with His disciples He promised them definitely a new life in which the power of the Spirit would enable them to live a life of obedience.

"But what becomes of man's sinful nature?" you ask. Man keeps his sinful nature to the end of his life. "In me (that is, in my flesh) nothing good dwells" (Rom. 7:18).

The Holy Spirit is the power of God that works within us, both to will and to do, and so prevents the flesh from gaining the upper hand. Think of the text in Hebrews 13:20–21: "The God of peace . . . make you complete in every good work to do His will, working in you what is well pleasing in His sight, through Jesus Christ."

Oh brother, these are no mere idle words: "If you love Me, keep My commandments," and "My Father will love him, and We will come to him and make Our home with him" (John 14:23). Believe that the Holy Spirit will cause the love of Christ to work in your heart in such power that you will be able to abide in the love of Jesus the whole day, and to keep His words with great joy. Then you will understand the saying: "This is the love of God, that we keep His commandments. And His commandments are not burdensome" (1 John 5:3). Only believe—that the Holy Spirit will endue you with power to live this life of perfect love.

Love and Prayer

Be serious and watchful in your prayers. And above all things have fervent love for one another.

First Peter 4:7–8

IN our text, watching unto prayer and fervent love are closely linked. This is true, too, in the spiritual life. The man who prays only for himself will not find it easy to be in the right attitude towards God. But where the heart is filled with fervent love to others, prayer will continually rise to God for those whom we love, and even for those with whom we do not agree.

There would be a great defect in this little book on brotherly love if we neglected to indicate what an important place prayer holds in the life of love. These two fruits of the Spirit are inseparably connected. If you wish your *love* to grow and increase, forget yourself and pray, pray earnestly, for God's children and His church. And if you would increase in *prayerfulness*, give yourself in fervent love to the service of those around you, helping to bear their burdens.

What a great need there is, at this time, for earnest, powerful intercessors! Let those who complain that there is so little love among Christians acknowledge that one of the chief signs of love is lacking in *themselves* if they do not pray much and often for their brethren. I am deeply convinced that God desires His children, as members of one body, to present themselves each day before the throne of grace to pray down the power of the Spirit upon all believers. Union is strength. This is true in regard to even the kingdom of heaven. Real spiritual unity will help us to forget ourselves; to live unselfishly, wholly for God and our fellow men. And the word of Peter will be applied to our lives—"watchful in prayer—fervent in love."

There can be no surer way of growing in the spirit of love than by uniting daily at the throne of grace and there finding our joy and life in a oneness of spirit with the whole body of Christ.

Let this little book on love be also a book on prayer. As we meditate on love to the brethren we shall be constrained to have fellowship with God. And we shall attain this, not by reading or thinking, but by communion with the Father and the Lord Jesus through the Holy Spirit. Love impels to prayer; to believing prayer is vouchsafed the love of God.

The First and Great Commandment

The LORD your God will circumcise your heart . . . to love the LORD your God with all your heart and with all your soul.

Deuteronomy 30:6

GOD greatly desires our love. It is the nature of all love to long to be acceptable and to meet with positive response. Yes, God longs with a never-ending, fervent desire to have our love, the love of the whole heart.

But how can I attain such a condition? Just in the same way that I receive salvation—through faith alone. Paul says: "I live by faith in the Son of God, who loved me" (Gal. 2:20). When we take time to wait upon God and remember with what a burning desire God sought to win our love—through the gift of His Son—we shall be able to realize that God has a strong and never-ceasing longing for the love of our heart.

Our hearts are blind and dark, and we are apt to forget that God longs each day for the love of His child. If I once begin to believe it, I shall feel constrained to tarry before God and ask Him to let His light shine into my heart. Just as the sun is willing to give me its light and heat if I will receive them, God is a thousand times more willing to give me the light and glow of His love. In the Old Testament God gave us the promise of the new covenant (Ezek. 36:25–26): "I will cleanse you . . . I will give you a new heart and put a new spirit within you."

He gave His Son to die for us in order to win our love. Take time, Oh my soul, to grasp this, and wait silently upon God and become strong in the assurance of faith: God, who longs for my love, is almighty, and will pour out His love in my heart through the Holy Spirit now dwelling within me.

Oh, that we could understand that there is nothing on earth to be compared to this experience! Shall I not take time each day and give God His desire, and believe with firmer faith? God, who so greatly longs for my love, will work within me by His Spirit, granting the desire to love Him with my whole heart and enabling me to prove my love by keeping His commandments.

Oh Lord, I bow before You; fulfill my longing desire—which is also Your desire— that my heart may be filled with Your love.

The Royal Law of Love

*If you really fulfill the royal law according to the Scripture,
"You shall love your neighbor as yourself," you do well.*

James 2:8

WHEN our Lord, in answer to the question "Teacher, which is the great commandment in the law?" (Matt. 22:36) had answered "You shall love the Lord your God with all your heart" (22:37), He added: "The second is like it: 'You shall love your neighbor as yourself'" (22:39). These two commandments both contain the one verb *love*. In heaven, where God is, and on earth among men, love is the royal law; love is supreme.

The Christian's love for his fellow men has more than one purpose:

1.   It reveals to us our own nature, implanted by God, that we should love ourselves; and it calls us to love our neighbors with the same love. It thereby affirms that there is in human hearts a divine law to love our neighbors as ourselves.

2.   Christianity teaches us to love our neighbor because God loves him. Every man, no matter how vile, has a share in God's compassion and love because he is made in God's image. I ought, then, to love my neighbor not merely because he is a fellow human, but because I see God's likeness in him and because God loves him. As God loves all men, even His enemies, even so—not more nor less—I must love *all*. "Be merciful, just as your

Father also is merciful" (Luke 6:36). From my Father in heaven I must learn how to love.

3.   The Christian's love of all mankind may rise still higher. In the realm of grace, God has reconciled us to Himself so that He can apportion to us His personal love. This is the law for each child of God: he must love his brother with the same love with which Christ has loved him.

4.   And then comes the last and the highest thought: that even as Christ in His great love redeemed a world dying in misery and sin, so all those who have received this love should give themselves likewise to love all men, devoting their lives to making others partakers of this great blessedness.

Child of God, here are four reasons why we should love our neighbor. Have they not a divine authority and irresistible power which will compel us to manifest this Christian love towards our brethren in fullness of beauty?

May God write the royal law of love deep in our hearts!

National Feeling

[God] has made from one blood every nation of men.

Acts 17:26

A former prime minister of England said in regard to the Boer War that it served to maintain the principle that smaller nationalities should not be oppressed. That is to say, that all these precious lives and the treasures of gold were offered up in a vindication of nationality, which may be regarded as a gift of God—as "the divine right of each nation, according to its special nature, to preserve and develop its individuality in the service of the common life of all the world." This war will develop national feeling more intensely, increase a national consciousness, and arouse hope amongst the peoples who have hitherto been considered the most backward in the world. People will slowly learn that national feeling depends on character, and character depends on religion.

"In a struggle such as this we cannot expect the breach to be healed at once; but we can cultivate a spirit of Christian sympathy with those who differ from us, and cease to regard each other with suspicion and distrust. We can trust the honesty of each other's convictions, and take more trouble to understand one another."

This extract speaks most strongly of the divine right of national feeling; yet we must also clearly understand that the feeling, as a merely human force, is under the power of *sin*. Let us remember that "every creature of God is good . . . for it is sanctified by the word of God and prayer" (1 Tim. 4:4–5). Without that sanctifying process, national feeling may become the prey of ambition and the source of hatred and aversion and contempt for other nations. God has, in Christ, placed all men under the law of *heavenly* love.

It is the holy calling of every Christian, and more especially of every minister of the gospel, under the guidance of the Holy Spirit to point out to others the way by which national feeling may attain its twofold aim: (1) the development and uplifting of the people themselves, and (2) the right attitude to other peoples in the upbuilding of all mankind.

One Stream or Two Streams?

*The stick . . . of Ephraim and . . . the stick of Judah, [I will]
make them one stick, and they will be one in My hand.*

Ezekiel 37:19

HERE in South Africa, nationalistic rivalry has been
the cause of much animosity and belligerence.
When the small stream of the Africander people, with
less than one million souls, was incorporated into the
mighty stream of the British Empire with its three hun-
dred millions, it was inevitable that this should happen.
But it is God's will that in the great stream there should
be two streams side by side. The two nationalities, the
smaller as well as the greater, have each their own history,
their own national characteristics, and their own special
virtues and shortcomings. In God's plan and council
there is room for both.

Why has there been such terrible strife and discord
over the question: One stream or two streams? Because
people would not accept both viewpoints and accord to
each its right. They wanted one or the other, exclusively,
in the foreground. They forgot that God had said: "What
God has joined together, let not man separate" (Matt.
19:6).

One who is really desirous of knowing and doing
God's will—in His dealings with our people—must try to
understand his twofold calling: to be faithful in preserving his own nationality, and at the same time to show

his love and appreciation of the second nationality, with whom, under God's providence, his lot has been cast.

God has given to His people in this land a great and holy calling: to prove, in submission to His will and in the power of His love, what it is to be a true Africander and yet at the same time a faithful subject of the British Empire. Our love to God and to our neighbors will supply the right incentive.

When Ephraim and Judah became one in God's hand, the difference between the two was not destroyed. Each kept his own characteristics. But the oneness was that of true unity and mutual love. "Ephraim shall not envy Judah, and Judah shall not harass Ephraim" (Isa. 11:13). God will fulfill this promise to us—but on one condition: We must place our people in God's hand by our prayers. "They will be one in My hand." Let us, by means of intercession, place our people in God's hand. He can, and will, give the love and mutual forbearance that is needed.

Pray for Love

The Lord make you increase and abound in love to one another and to all, just as we do to you, so that He may establish your hearts blameless in holiness.

First Thessalonians 3:12–13

WHAT a prayer! That the Lord would make them to abound in love towards each other, even as Paul did towards them: that He would strengthen their hearts to be unblameable in holiness. Without love, this was impossible. Only by the power of God could their hearts be strengthened for a life of true holiness and of love to the brethren. Let us use this prayer often, both for ourselves and for those around us. Do you pray for holiness? Then show it by a hearty love to the brethren!

In Second Thessalonians 3:5 we read: "The Lord direct your hearts into the love of God." Yes, that is what the Lord Jesus will do for us—give us a heart always directed to the love of God. Lord, by Your great love, grant me a heart of love!

"Always in every prayer of mine making request for you all with joy . . . I pray, that your love may abound still more and more in knowledge . . . that you may be . . . filled with the fruits of righteousness" (Phil. 1:4, 9–11). The apostle, in his constant prayer for those in his charge, makes love the chief thing. Let us do the same.

"I want you to know what a great conflict I have for you that [your] hearts may be encouraged, being knit together in love, and attaining to all riches of the full assurance of understanding" (Col. 2:1–2). Paul considers it indispensable for the believers' growth in the knowledge of God that their hearts should be knit together in love. God is love—everlasting, endless love. That love can only be experienced when Christians are knit together in love and live for others, and not only for themselves.

These four prayers of Paul give us abundant matter for meditation and prayer. Take time to let these heavenly thoughts grow in your heart. As the sun freely gives its light and heat to the grass and grain, that they may grow and bring forth fruit, so God is far more willing to give His love to us in ever-increasing measure. Oh Christian, if you feel as if you cannot pray, take these words of divine love and ponder them in your heart. You will gain a strong and a joyous assurance of what God is able to do for you. He will make you to abound in love and strengthen your heart to live before Him in holiness and love to the brethren.

Lord, teach me so to pray!

Like Christ

I have given you an example, that you should do as I have done to you.

John 13:15

THE love of Christ, manifested in His death on the cross, is not only the ground of our hope of salvation but it is the only rule for our daily life and conduct. Our Lord says clearly: "You should do as I have done." The love of Christ is my only hope of salvation. A walk in that love is the way truly and fully to *enjoy* that salvation.

"Let each of us please his neighbor for his good, leading to edification. For even Christ did not please Himself. . . . Therefore receive one another, just as Christ also received us" (Rom. 15:2–3, 7). God will work the power within us to "receive one another, just as Christ also received us." He will do it for every upright soul and for all who pray in confident faith.

"Therefore be imitators of God as dear children. And walk in love, as Christ also has loved us and given Himself for us" (Eph. 5:1–2). Here again, *love* is everything. We must realize that Christ loved us even unto death, and that we are now God's dear children. It follows naturally that we should *walk* in love. Those who keep close to Christ *will* walk in love.

"Therefore, as the elect of God, holy and beloved, put on tender mercies . . . bearing with one another, and forgiving one another . . . even as Christ forgave you, so you also must do. But above all these things put on love, which is the bond of perfection" (Col. 3:12–14). What a blessed life is possible because of the love and the power that we have in Christ! What a blessed walk in His fellowship is ours when we are led by the Holy Spirit and strengthened for a life in His likeness!

Oh God, the Father of love, the Father of Christ, our Father, will You indeed strengthen us each day to love one another in Christ, even as He loved us!

The Power of God's Word

The words that I speak to you are spirit, and they are life.
John 6:63

You received the word of God . . . as it is in truth, the word of God, which also effectively works in you who believe.
First Thessalonians 2:13

The word of God is living and powerful.
Hebrews 4:12

THE question constantly recurs: What is the reason that God's children so little realize the great value and absolute necessity of brotherly love? One answer is: because of their unbelief. Without faith, great faith, persevering faith, there can be no realization of the power of love within us. This is a different faith from what we usually mean when we say we believe in God's Word. This true faith is deeper and higher. It bows before God in a deep realization of His greatness, of His power to work wonders in our hearts, and of His loving care for us. The word of a king or of a general has great influence over his soldiers. And how great beyond compare is the Word of the infinite and almighty One!

It is necessary to be deeply convinced of our utter inability to produce this love, which is holy and can conquer sin and unbelief. We need a burning desire to receive this heavenly love into our hearts whatever the cost may be. Then at length we shall gain an insight into what God's Word is as a living power in our hearts. This supernatural power will be the love of God poured out in our hearts by the Holy Spirit living and working within us.

In the following daily portion we shall consider verses from the first epistle of John, verses in which the love of God is promised to believers. Let each Christian ask himself if he is ready to acknowledge his deep sinfulness and lack of power and to yield his heart unreservedly for this love to take possession. But above all, let him take time in God's presence to wait on Him in confidence that His Word will work effectually in us as a seed of new life. Then we shall love our Lord Jesus and our brethren with a love like that with which God has loved us.

Perfect Love According to 1 John

These are the true sayings of God.

Revelation 19:9

He who loves his brother abides in the light.

First John 2:10

"WHOEVER does not practice righteousness is not of God, nor is he who does not love his brother. For this is the message that you heard from the beginning, that we should love one another" (1 John 3:10–11). "We know that we have passed from death to life, because we love the brethren" (3:14). "By this we know love, because He laid down His life for us. And we also ought to lay down our lives for the brethren" (3:16). "And this is His commandment: that we should believe on the name of His Son Jesus Christ, and love one another" (3:23). "Beloved, let us love one another; for love is of God" (4:7). "Beloved, if God so loved us, we also ought to love one another. . . . If we love one another, God abides in us, and His love has been perfected in us. . . . We have known and believed the love that God has for us. God is love, and he who abides in love abides in God, and God in him" (4:11–12, 16). "If someone says, 'I love God,' and hates his brother, he is a liar; for he who does not love his brother whom he has seen, how can he love God whom he has not seen? And this commandment we have from Him: that he who loves God must love his brother also" (4:20–21).

Each of these words is a living seed and has within it a divine power, and so is able to take root and grow and bear fruit in our hearts. But just as a seed requires that the soil in which it grows be kept free of all weeds, so the heart must be wholly surrendered to God and His service in order that the seed of the Word may bear this heavenly fruit.

Read over again First John 3:23. As necessary as faith is for our salvation, so necessary is love of the brethren. And (see 4:21) love to God and love to the brethren are inseparable.

The Love that Suffers

Walk in love, as Christ also has loved us and given Himself for us.

Ephesians 5:2

IS it not strange that love, which is the source of the greatest happiness, should also be the cause of the most intense suffering? Our life on earth is such that suffering is always involved, for love seeks to save the object of its love. Yes, it is only by means of suffering that love can gain its end and so attain the highest happiness.

What a wonderful thought! Even the almighty power of God's love could not achieve its purpose without suffering which passes understanding. By means of His sufferings, Christ bore and overcame the sins of the whole world, and the hard heart of man was softened and drawn to God. So love in the midst of suffering manifested the greatest glory and attained its end perfectly.

Let no one, with such an example before him, imagine that love is self-sufficient. No. Love worthy of the name manifests itself in a life of continual self-sacrifice. Love's strength lies in renunciation. Just think what a mother suffers when a beloved child is ill, or when a son falls into evil ways. Love gives her strength to endure, whatever the circumstances may be. Think, too, what one must undergo who has yielded himself wholeheartedly to work and to pray for others. It may mean tears and heartache, and much wrestling in prayer. But love overcomes all obstacles.

Oh Christian, do you really long to know the love of Christ in all its fullness? Then yield yourself wholly to Him and His blessed service. Regard yourself as a channel through which the Highest Love can attain His aim. Take the souls around you into a sympathizing, loving heart, and begin to suffer with them and intercede for them. Let it be your chief delight to live and to suffer for others, in the love and fellowship of the Lord Jesus. Then at length you will realize what this life of love is as a servant of God—and, even as God Himself and as Christ, will live wholly for the welfare and happiness of others.

Oh soul, dwell on this wondrous truth, that there can be no real fellowship in the love of Christ save in unreserved surrender to seek always the glory of God in the salvation of your fellow men. "He who abides in love abides in God, and God in him" (1 John 4:16).

The Works of the Flesh

The works of the flesh are evident, which are: . . . sorcery, hatred, contentions, jealousies, outbursts of wrath . . . envy, murders . . . and the like.

Galatians 5:19–21

PAUL in these three verses mentions seventeen of the terrible "works of the flesh." Nine of these are sins against love. And he says elsewhere (Eph. 4:31), "Let all bitterness, wrath, anger, clamor, and evil speaking be put away from you, with all malice." He here answers the question why there is so little love among Christians, and why it is so hard to arouse such love. All these sins are "works of the flesh."

Even the earnest Christian is still in the flesh. Paul says: "In me (that is, in my flesh) nothing good dwells" (Rom. 7:18); "Because the carnal mind is enmity against God" (8:7). It is quite impossible for a Christian by his own efforts to lead a life of love.

Scripture says: "Walk in the Spirit, and you shall not fulfill the lust of the flesh" (Gal. 5:16). The Spirit will enable us to keep the flesh always in subjection. The "fruit of the Spirit" will be Christ's love poured into our hearts as a fountain of love. Paul adds to what was quoted above: "The law of the Spirit of life in Christ Jesus has made me free from the law of sin" (Rom. 8:2). The grace of God will enable the Christian to walk, not after the flesh, but after the Spirit.

Learn these three great lessons: (1) The Christian cannot in his own strength love God and his fellow man. (2) The great reason for so much bitterness and lack of love is that the Christian walks after the flesh. (3) The only sure way to abide in this life of love—to love God and Christ with the whole heart, to love the brethren fervently, and to have a tender, compassionate love for all who do not yet know Christ—is an absolute surrender to the Holy Spirit, to be led and guided by Him each day of our lives. It is through the Holy Spirit that this love is poured out in our hearts.

Child of God, learn the lesson that the Holy Spirit will take entire possession of you and will work continually within you a life of love to Christ and to all men. Pray over this thought until it gains control of your whole being!

Passing the Love of Women

*My brother Jonathan; You have been very pleasant to me;
Your love to me was wonderful, Surpassing the love of
women.*

Second Samuel 1:26

GOD created man in order to show what power love
has: for example, when a man strives for the welfare
of others and even gives up his life for them. He created
woman, however, to show what tenderness and quiet
endurance are: as when she sacrifices herself for the sake
of others. A little child, during the first years of its life, is
dependent on the mother. This is not only that the child
may learn to love its mother, but that the mother herself
may be trained in the school of self-sacrificing love—for
her greatest adorning is "the incorruptible beauty of a
gentle and quiet spirit, which is very precious in the sight
of God" (1 Pet. 3:4).

The tendency nowadays in public life is to place
woman on an equal footing with man. This is only
right in many cases. But one must not forget that the
best ornament of a woman is a meek and quiet spirit,
which is of great price in the sight of God and of man,
and which makes her a blessing in her home. It is the
suffering, prayerful, all-conquering love of the wife and
the mother which secures the happiness of a people.

Dear sisters, preserve as a great treasure the precious
jewel which God has entrusted to you—to reflect the love

of God in all its tenderness and sympathy. "As one whom his mother comforts, So I will comfort you" (Isa. 66:13). Let each one, as she reads this book, take time to meditate on God's wonderful love and pray for it earnestly in a receptive spirit. This will give her a heavenly influence and power over her husband and children, and in her dealings with her neighbors she will be a living witness to what the love of God can do.

Think of Mary, the woman who loved much, and the other women to whom the Lord revealed Himself on the resurrection morning. It was the love of these women that gave them the right to be the first to meet the Lord and to take the message to the disciples.

God bless the mothers and wives and daughters of our land! May they prove in their lives how beautiful and powerful the love of women is! And the words from the time of David will still be true: "Surpassing the love of women" is the love of God's children.

Stewards of the Love of God

Let a man so consider us, as servants of Christ and stewards of the mysteries of God. Moreover it is required in stewards that one be found faithful.

First Corinthians 4:1–2

A steward is a man to whom a king or master entrusts his treasures and goods in order to apportion them to those who have a right to them. God in heaven needs men on earth to make known the treasures of His love and to give them to those who have need. Each minister of the gospel is a steward of the mystery of God and, above all, of the deep mystery of His everlasting love and all the blessings that flow from it.

It is required in stewards that a man be found faithful; he must devote himself wholly to his life task. He must be faithful at his work, and always at his post in the palace or house where the treasures are stored up. So the minister of the gospel must himself be faithful, living each day in the love and fellowship of God. He must be faithful not only to God but to his fellow men, caring for the needs of the souls entrusted to him and ready to recommend God's love and to share it with others. This divine love is a mystery, and can only dwell in a heart set apart for God and satisfied with His love, which flows from Him as a stream of living water.

Oh child of God, seek to have a deeper insight into what the office of a servant of God means, as a steward of the wonderful love of God to sinners. Pray much and often for your ministers that God may hide them in the secret of His tabernacle, so that they may be faithful stewards of the mystery of God, and chiefly of the mystery of divine love.

And you, my beloved brethren, to whom the love of God in heaven and of Christ on the cross is entrusted, remember that your congregation, your church, your people, are dependent on your faithfulness in living a heavenly life in fellowship with God. Then you will be able with joy, and in the power of the Holy Spirit, to pass on the love of God to souls that so greatly need it.

Faith Working Through Love

In Christ Jesus neither circumcision nor uncircumcision
avails anything, but faith working through love.

Galatians 5:6

FAITH is the root: Love is the fruit. Faith becomes strong in the love of God and of Christ. Faith in God and love to the brethren must always go hand in hand. Faith in God's wonderful love, poured out in our hearts, enables us to live always in love towards our fellow men. This true faith gives us power for a life of fervent, all-embracing love. Yet how little the church realizes of all this! How seldom does the preacher lay stress on a Christlike love to the brethren as the fruit and joy of the life of faith!

All of our life—in the home, between father and mother, parents and children, brothers and sisters, friends and servants—should be a life in the love of Christ. Do not say: "It is impossible." All things are possible to God, who through His Holy Spirit will pour His love in our hearts to be lived out in our daily lives. Let our faith cling to God's Word, and to the unseen and wonderful things He will do for us each day. Let these thoughts about love impel us to accept with new and greater faith the love of God, and then dedicate our lives to letting it radiate from us to all men, yes, even to our enemies, and to the heathen at the uttermost parts of the earth.

Oh Christian, the whole of salvation lies in these two words: *faith* and *love*. Let our faith each day take deeper root in God's eternal love. And then each day the fruit of the Spirit will be love in all our dealings with those around us. May God imprint these words deeply in our hearts, and make them a joy and strength to us: In Jesus Christ nothing avails but "faith working through love."

PRAYERS

Thanksgiving

OUR Father, who art in heaven, we worship You as the eternal, unsearchable, glorious Fount, from which Your love fills earth and heaven. Your name be the glory to all eternity!

We thank You, with unspeakable joy, for the revelation of that love on the cross of Your beloved Son, and for the blood wherewith He has bought and redeemed us to walk before You as the children of Your love.

We thank You for the gift of the Holy Spirit to pour out Your love in our hearts, in all its sustaining and preserving power.

We thank You for this love as it flows from us, in love to the brethren, in love to all men, yes, in love to those who hate and despise us.

Oh our Father, grant to us, as Your dear children, the heirs of Your love, to walk with You on earth, and then in the full manifestation of Your love to dwell with You to all eternity. For Christ's sake. Amen.

Confession of Sin

OUR Father, we bow before You in deep humility at the thought of Your unsearchable love, and the love of Christ which passes all knowledge. Oh God, we are filled with shame at the thought that we so little know Your love, and so little desire to know it. You have given us the highest proof of Your love in the love of Christ our Lord on the cross, and yet we so little love You in return.

Yea, Lord, we repent in dust and ashes that we love You so little, and do not live to Your honor and glory. We so little manifest that fervent love to the brethren by which the world would know that we are Christ's disciples, and yet You love us with a share of the same love wherewith You have loved Your Son.

Oh God, we beseech You, pour out Your Spirit upon Your church, and the power of Your love into our hearts, through the Holy Spirit. And grant that throughout the world witnesses may be found to publish with divine power, by word and deed: God is Love; God is Love. Amen.

Supplication

OUR Father, the God of Love, who desires to make each of Your children a bearer of that love unto others and a shining light before men, we humbly pray You, let that love take full possession of us. Lord God, Your love is so endless, so mighty, so willing to take possession of us and through us to manifest its power. We pray You, let that love have full sway in our hearts. Draw us to Yourself, that we may continue in prayer and delight in fellowship with You until the eternal love takes full control, and enables us to show, day by day, that in Christ Jesus nothing avails but faith working by love.

Oh Lord, we beseech You most earnestly, deliver us from our blindness, our selfishness, our uncharitableness. Yes, Lord, may Your love become ours, so that we may yield ourselves to live wholeheartedly in and for that love. Amen.

Intercession

OUR Father, we would pray not only for ourselves but for Your children throughout the whole world. We implore You, Father, our Father, pour out Your love in the hearts of Your people. Remove all self-confidence and unbelief, and grant Your servants a vision of what true faith means—the power of a love which lives for others.

Hear our prayer for our own church. Hear our prayer for all other churches. Hear our prayer for Your church all over the world. Oh God, let Your light shine forth and the glory of the Lord be upon her, that she may find her chief joy in self-sacrificing love.

Hear us for our ministers, for all ministers, that they may have such an experience of Your love as to proclaim the gospel with power, that all may know that the life of God in the soul is rooted in a love that passes knowledge, flowing forth to all around us. For Christ's sake. Amen.

Fort Washington, PA 19034

This book is published by CLC Publications, an outreach of CLC
Ministries International. The purpose of CLC is to make evangelical
Christian literature available to all nations so that people may come
to faith and maturity in the Lord Jesus Christ. We hope this book has
been life changing and has enriched your walk with God through the
work of the Holy Spirit. If you would like to know more about CLC,
we invite you to visit our website:

www.clcusa.org

To know more about the remarkable story of the founding of
CLC International we encourage you to read

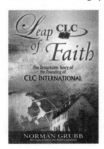

LEAP OF FAITH

Norman Grubb

Paperback
Size 5¹/₄ x 8, Pages 248
ISBN: 978-0-87508-650-7
ISBN (e-book): 978-1-61958-055-8

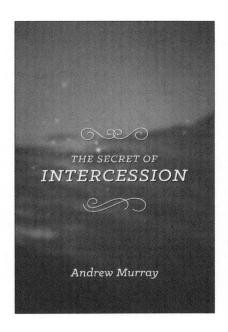

THE SECRET OF INTERCESSION

Andrew Murray

The Secret Series books contain a wealth of teaching that is based on Andrew Murray's mature and full experience in Christ. *The Secret of Intercession* contains one month of daily selections that reveal the power of intercession.

Paperback
Size 4¹/₄ x 7, Pages 67
ISBN: 978-1-61958-249-1
ISBN (*e-book*): 978-1-61958-250-7

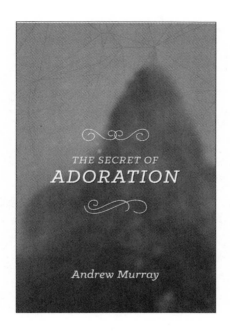

THE SECRET OF ADORATION

Andrew Murray

The Secret Series books contain a wealth of teaching that is based on Andrew Murray's mature and full experience in Christ. *The Secret of Adoration* contains one month of daily selections that highlight the importance of true worship in the lives of believers.

Paperback
Size 4¹/₄ x 7, Pages 71
ISBN: 978-1-61958-253-8
ISBN (*e-book*): 978-1-61958-254-5